# It's That Easy

A Struggling Christian's Guide
to Walking in Victory!

PRISCILLA WRIGHT

Copyright © 2024 Priscilla Wright
All rights reserved
First Edition

NEWMAN SPRINGS PUBLISHING
320 Broad Street
Red Bank, NJ 07701

First originally published by Newman Springs Publishing 2024

All biblical citations were taken from the New King James Version of the Holy Bible.

ISBN 979-8-89308-777-2 (Paperback)
ISBN 979-8-89308-778-9 (Digital)

Printed in the United States of America

I dedicate this book to my daughter Briana for inspiring me to follow my dream, your love and support means everything to me.

# Contents

Introduction..................................................................vii

| Part 1: | Sin ...........................................................1 |
| Chapter 1: | What Is Sin?............................................3 |
| | How to Avoid Sin....................................4 |
| | Can You Be Delivered from Sin? ............5 |

| Part 2: | The Process ...........................................9 |
| Chapter 2: | What Is the Process?..............................11 |
| | Will the Process Be Hard? .....................12 |

| Part 3: | Who Are You?......................................15 |
| Chapter 3: | Knowing Who You Are .........................17 |
| | Looking at Self......................................18 |
| | Changing How You Think ....................19 |

| Part 4: | The Path ..............................................23 |
| Chapter 4: | The Road Won't Be Easy ......................25 |
| | Adversities ............................................26 |
| | Know Your Enemy ...............................27 |

| Part 5: | The Steps .............................................31 |
| Chapter 5: | Walking by Faith ..................................33 |
| | Power and Authority ............................34 |
| | Victory .................................................36 |

# Introduction

# The Struggle

*Struggle* is a word that means "to make a forceful or violent effort to get free of restraints or constriction." How often do you struggle as a born-again, Bible-carrying Christian? Yes, the struggle is real for believing Christians, who are in a constant battle with their enemies. The devil and self are two of the worst enemies to fight each and every day—the devil, with his mental attacks, and self, with fleshy desires.

How can you win these battles? It's not hard when you walk in the process. For some, the process will be hard, and for others, it will be a little easier, no matter where you are in your Christian walk. I pray that you will receive something that will encourage you and help in your Christian development. In this book, I have outlined chapters and given snippets of my own struggles I have overcame, I pray it will help you understand why you are struggling as a believer and how to walk in *victory*.

# Part 1

# Sin

## Chapter 1

# What Is Sin?

What is *sin*? Sin is an immoral act considered to be a transgression against divine law.

Synonyms: *wrongdoing, act of evil, wickedness, crime, offense, misdeed, misdemeanor, misbehave, to go astray.*

As Christians, you are to avoid sin, even the very look of it.

> Abstain from all appearance of evil.
> (1 Thessalonians 5:22)

The Bible lists some sins that, as Christians, you have been guilty of committing before you were saved or you might be struggling with some of these sins right now.

1. Unrighteous—wicked, evil doing.
2. Fornicators—sex between unmarried couples.
3. Adulterers—married person having sex not with spouse.
4. Idolaters—people worshiping things other than God.
5. Effeminate—a male identifying with women characteristics.
6. Abusers of themselves with mankind—same-sex relations.
7. Thieves—a person taking things without permission.
8. Covetous—eagerly desirous wealth or possessions, greedy.
9. Drunkard—a person who drinks excessively.
10. Revilers—to speak abusively, cussing.

These are some that are listed in 1 Corinthians 6:9–10. I have found in my Christian walk that a lot of believers did or do not know the meaning of some of the sins they were engaging in. I had people in my Bible study class ask me, "What is that, or what does that mean?" I gave one example of unrighteous behavior: Listening to a coworker tell a dirty joke, and as a Christian, you laugh and continue to engage—that would be considered unrighteous behavior.

There are other sins the Bible speaks about, and these are just a few. All sins are the same in the eyesight of God. They all separate you from God, so do not violate your conscience by doing those things that are against your character. The Bible tells us that we were all born in sin and have a sin nature.

> And you he made alive, who were dead in trespasses and sins. (Ephesians 2:1)

> And such were some of you: but ye are washed, but ye are sanctified, but ye are justified in the name of the Lord Jesus, and by the spirit of God. (1 Corinthians 6:11)

Jesus paid the penalty for your sins and the sins of the whole world on the cross, so you must repent and turn away from the sin or sins you are struggling in.

## How to Avoid Sin

There are a number of ways to avoid sin, and one way would be to be mindful of the people you are in friendships with. You must not hang around people who are engaging in sinful activities that would entice you to fall back into your sinful ways and lifestyle.

> My son if sinners entice thee, consent though not. (Proverbs 1:10)

That was the problem I had—hanging around friends who wanted to go out to bars and clubs. And after I became a Christian, I would try to continue to go out with them. But I would start feeling bad after I got home, and I didn't know why. One day, I was reading the Bible, and it started to make sense why I was not having fun anymore going out with my friends.

> For they that are after the flesh do mind the things of the flesh, but they that are after the spirit the things of the spirit. For to be carnally minded is death, but to be spiritually minded is life and peace. (Romans 8:5–6)

I had to learn to walk in the spirit so I would not have the desire to seek the things of the flesh. Be mindful of the things you watch on TV and listen to on the radio. The content can also cause you to fall backward in your walk with the Lord. Cussing and sexual contents on the television shows can lead you astray. Understand that the devil's job is to pull you back into your old sinful ways. He comes to kill, steal, and destroy you and your testimony.

> Be sober, be vigilant because your adversary the devil walks about like a roaring lion, seeking whom he may devour. (1 Peter 5:8)

Allow the Holy Spirit to guide and direct you in your walk with the Lord. The Holy Spirit now lives in you; he is the comforter of whom Jesus spoke of. We are to feed the spirit and deny our fleshly desires.

## Can You Be Delivered from Sin?

*Yes*. When you turn away from those sins and stop trying to deliver yourself, give all those sins you are struggling with to God, he can take care of you. His son, Jesus, took all your sins on the cross so you don't have to struggle with them any longer. God wants to be in every area of your life; he can handle everything that is causing his children pain and discomfort. He knows everything about you.

> Being confident of this very thing, that He who began a good work in you will complete it until the day of Jesus Christ. (Philippians 1:6)

Christians you do not have to live in bondage or be double-minded in you walk with the Lord. That kind of confused thinking is caused by the devil and his cohorts. You are free; you were free when you accepted Jesus into your life. But the enemy wants you to believe that you must work at freeing yourself and that if you mess up or fall, you are no longer a child of God or loved by him. That is a lie from the pits of hell.

> Therefore if the Son makes you free, you shall be free indeed. (John 8:36)

> Therefore submit to God, resist the devil and he will flee from you. Draw near to God and he will draw near to you. Cleanse your hands, you sinners; and purify your hearts, you double minded. (James 4:7–8)

## IT'S THAT EASY

Discussed your thoughts for the chapter and write your own prayer.

# Part 2

# The Process

# Chapter 2

# What Is the Process?

The process began when you acknowledged you needed Jesus and couldn't do this walk without God. I thought I could do this walk alone, but I could not stop falling and messing up. I was always discouraged and telling people how hard it was to be a Christian. It all started to change when I committed myself to reading the Bible. It was then that I started confessing my faults and repenting of my sins, and that's what you will have to do as a struggling Christian: Commit to repentance and confession of your sins and allow God to start the process in you.

> For with the heart one believes unto righteousness, and with the mouth confession is made unto salvation. (Romans 10:10)

It is very important that you stay in the Word of God (Bible), praying and asking God for wisdom and direction. When you are struggling in your walk, you cannot walk the process successfully by ignoring God and his Word. When I was struggling, I asked God for wisdom to help me navigate through the Word.

> If any of you lacks wisdom, let him ask of God. who gives to all liberally and without reproach, and it will be given to him. (James 1:5)

## Will the Process Be Hard?

If you have a willing heart and mind, it will be a lot easier than if you're sitting on both sides of the fence, unable to make up your mind as to whether you should surrender totally to the Lord or hold on to some of your ungodly ways. Your goal is to be Christlike and turn away from old behaviors and habits that keep you from having a relationship with the Almighty God. Do not make excuses or accept sinful behavior by thinking, *That is just how it is*, or *I was born like this so I can't change or be changed*. That is a lie of the devil. Even if you have some discouraging moments, never give up; just keep trusting in God and building upon your faith.

> Though he fall, he shall not be utterly cast down; for the Lord upholds him with His hand. (Psalm 37:24)

> For a righteous man may fall seven times and rise again. But the wicked shall fall by calamity. (Proverbs 24:16)

Never fight against the process because of the spirit of pride. Do not try to hold on to friends and family members who are keeping you in sinful relationships and behaviors. Remember that you are to worship the Creator and not his creations. There should never be anything in a Christian's life that you can't give up for the love and relationship of Christ. Our relationship with family and friends that are not Christians is not to be mean to them, but if they are causing you to walk away from your faith, you must let them go. A Christian's job is to always lead unbelievers to Christ, not away. Your light is always to shine brighter in this world, so unbelievers WILL want to have what you have, and that is a relationship with God. Never fool yourself into thinking that you alone can pull unbelievers out of sinful behavior. The devil knows how to pull you back into the world quicker than you can pull a sinner out because you are struggling in your walk. Never try to take on the devil on his turf.

> Can two walk together except they are agreed? (Amos 3:3)

The process is to believe that God loves you that he wants the best for you, so embrace the process and allow God to do the work in your life and give him the opportunity to bring people and things in your life that will be beneficial to your growth and development as a Christian. Once you start to truly commit to the process, you will begin to find it hard to be around friends and family that are cussing and telling dirty jokes. I found it hard to continue to be around my friends and family members once I fully committed myself to walk with the Lord. I no longer wanted to go to bars and clubs or hear people talk dirty. I had no interest or desire to do those things I used to do. God had begun to change me from the inside out once I stopped trying to change myself.

PRISCILLA WRIGHT

Discussed your thoughts for the chapter and write your own prayer.

# Part 3

# Who Are You?

# Chapter 3

# Knowing Who You Are

It is very important to know who you are in Christ Jesus, knowing that you are a child of God and that he loves you, it will help you to begin seeing yourself differently and conducting yourself in a better way. As Christians, you are not to be acting like the world in words or deeds. God called you a peculiar people, and that means unusual.

> But ye are a chosen generation, a royal priesthood, a holy nation, His own special people, that you may proclaim the Praises of Him who called you out of darkness into His marvelous light. (1 Peter 2:9)

When you know who you are, you will begin to conduct yourself in a different way. You will become more humbled, and you will walk in confidence and have a boldness as David had when he went up against Goliath or Daniel when he didn't bow down to the king. They had a boldness because they trusted in God, and they knew who they were. They were the children of the Most High God, and they had assurance in their God that he would do what they said he would do. That is the kind of faith and trust as Christians you should have—a blind faith that whatever you ask in faith, you will receive. You will begin to know what and how to ask God for whatever you need; no longer will you be focused on yourself. The closer you get to the Father, your priorities will change, and you will want to be a blessing to others and have a closer relationship with God.

> Trust in the Lord with all your heart, and lean
> not on your own understanding. (Proverbs 3:5)

## Looking at Self

Walking with the Lord will cause you to look at yourself and examine where you are in your journey. You will begin to look at those things and people in your life that are keeping you from living a full and productive life. At this point, it's time to let God know everything and talk to God about all your faults and shortcomings and weaknesses and unconfessed sins that you think you are hiding from him. (FYI, he already knows.)

When I started confessing, I didn't just confess to anyone; I confessed everything I had ever done to my Aunt Hazel, who I knew was a strong, faithful woman of God. Even though I was still struggling I knew I needed someone with whom I could trust, and that is exactly what you will need to do. Find someone who you trust and who can pray with you and for you during those difficult times when you feel weak and alone. (Hopefully, it will be another Christian). Doing self-examination will reveal how God is working on you. When you start to see sin for what it truly is and you no longer want to make excuses for bad behavior, the sins you are struggling with will become less of a struggle.

When I started getting closer in my relationship with the Father, I took stock in my friendships, asking myself the questions, "Are these people benefiting me in my walk with Christ? Are they blocking me from receiving from God?" I started seeing God remove people and things out of my life, and it was truly amazing to see how fast he began to move things around for me.

> If we confess our sins, he is faithful and
> just to forgive us our sins and cleanse us from all
> unrighteousness. (1 John 1:9)

# IT'S THAT EASY

## Changing How You Think

After you have examined yourself and find that you are still struggling with some sins that have become a strong hold, you might want to evaluate how you see the world and the people in it because in order to change your behavior, you must change your mindset. How you see things and people will have a lot to do with how you behave and love. You will not love others or even serve others if you see them as different from you, whether it's their color or gender. This can cause you not to walk as a true Christian. Change your mind, then you can change your walk.

> And do not be conformed to this world, but be transformed by the renewing of your mind, that you may prove what is that good and acceptable and perfect will of God. (Romans 12:2)

> Let love be without Hypocrisy. Abhor what is evil. Cling to what is good. Be kindly affectionate to one another with brotherly love, in honor giving preference to one another. (Romans 12:9–10)

When you became a born-again believer, your spirit man changed not your flesh or soul; they had already been programmed from the day you were born. Remember, we all were born in sin and have a sin nature, so everything you started learning after birth were from your parents or other adults. What you saw and heard was what you learned, whether it was good or bad; all was programmed in you. When you became a Christian, the Holy Spirit came in, and your spirit man got a brand-new start but not your flesh or soul. That's why you still act and think the way you do, and the only way to change is to be reprogrammed, and that is by reading the Word of God and finding out what God says about how you are to conduct yourself as becoming a Christian in this world. How you should see your fellow man, how to show love to others, how to conduct yourself in business, how to raise children, and how to handle money matters—all of this will be found in the Word of God.

Building a closer relationship with God will cause you to read the Bible more, praise, pray, and worship more; and before long, your way of thinking will change.

Another important factor in changing the way you think is changing how you see God. Some see God as a punisher ready to strike you down at the first sign of wrongdoing or see God as unreachable. God is love; he loves his children and wants the best for you. In my walk, I found it hard to believe that God loved me, a struggling Christian who kept messing up. I couldn't grasp that he loved me until one day, I just sat and kept repeating to myself that God loves me. I don't know how many times I said it or how long I said it, but I said it until something clicked. I began to see myself as loved by God. No longer did I have pity parties when I messed up; I just stayed in the Word.

> There is therefore now no condemnation to those who are in Christ Jesus, who do not walk according to the flesh, but according to the spirit. (Romans 8:1)

When you know that God loves you, it will open up your heart and mind to receive from him, and you will see things as God sees them. Our goal is to be Christlike, and that means having the mind of Christ. When you change your thinking, you will change your behavior.

## IT'S THAT EASY

Discussed your thoughts for the chapter and write your own prayer.

# Part 4

# The Path

# Chapter 4

# The Road Won't Be Easy

Have you ever heard the expression, "The road won't be easy," or something similar to it? Well, that is a true statement. During your journey with the Lord, you will have tests, trials, and tribulations. But don't give up. It will be for your growth and development. Don't fall apart when you encounter obstacles and things you don't understand; all will be a learning experience.

> Beloved, do not think it strange concerning the fiery trials which is to try you, as though some strange thing happened unto you, but rejoice, to the extent that you partake of Christ's sufferings, that when His glory is revealed, you may also be glad with exceeding joy. (1 Peter 4:12–13)

Do not suffer because of wrongdoings or because you are living an unrighteous lifestyle. That will only make your walk with Christ harder because you are causing your own struggle. As a born-again believer, you are to suffer for doing the will of God.

> Yet if anyone suffers as a Christian, let him not be ashamed but let him glorify God in this matter. (1 Peter 4:16)

Know that God loves you and has promised to never leave you nor forsake you. He will be with you during your walk, so there is no need to fall apart at the first signs of trouble. Know that whatever the situation, it will always be for your good. It is a learning experience to help you in your faith and to show you how you are. Keep moving forward. You may not know when your test or trial will come, but know that they will come.

Remember to not fall apart or fall away from God. Do not start blaming God because that's what the devil wants you to do in order to pull you back into your old sinful ways and habits. Don't let the devil use you. Stay focused and know that good will come from whatever you go through.

> And not only that, but we also glory in tribulations, knowing that tribulation produces perseverance; and perseverance, character; and character, hope. Now hope does not disappoint, because the love of God has been poured out in our hearts by the Holy Spirit who was given to us. (Romans 5:3–5)

God wants you to succeed in your walk with him. He knows that you have moments where you struggle and fall short. He is not surprised by anything that you do, but he wants you to push on to the prize and get stronger in his Word and continue to learn from your tests and trials along the way. The road is not to be traveled alone. Get with other believers and join Bible study groups. This will all help you build a solid foundation. I was blessed to have a Christian aunt to help and teach me how to properly read the Bible and pray. Having that support is important when walking with the Lord.

## Adversities

What are *adversities*? They are difficulties, misfortunes, troubles, and hardships. Adversities will come into the life of a believer in three ways.

1. God (John 9:1–7)
2. Devil (Job 1:1–8)
3. Self (James 1:13–14)

When God puts you through the fire of adversities, it is for the purpose of getting your attention, to lead you into self-examination and also to change your behavior or belief. Adversities can bring you to a higher level of understanding. It can change your perception or view of the world and the people in it. The devil brings adversities to tear down your faith and belief in God, to get you to go back to your sinful ways, to destroy your character as a Christian, and to kill your spirit. Sin of self is when you are tempted by your own lustful ways in which you cause your own adversities. Pride will also cause adversities in your life, thinking you can defeat sin on your own. Your response to any form of adversity should always lead you to confession and repentance.

I learned the hard way that when adversities come, complaining, getting upset, and allowing my emotions to take over caused me a lot of heartache, and it did not do any good. It only caused me to stay in the situation a lot longer. I had to learn to go through with humility and grace, have an understanding that it was for my good, and use it as my testimony. Allow the Holy Spirit to direct you in your walk with the Lord and stay in the Word of God to keep you focused on him and not the problems.

> I say then; walk in the Spirit, and you shall
> not fulfill the lust of the flesh. (Galatians 5:16)

## Know Your Enemy

We know that the main enemy of a child of God is the devil. Some Christians do not believe that the devil or demons are real; some would like to believe that God or themselves are responsible for the good or bad that happens in their lives. This is not so. The devil also plays a role in what happens in a believer's life. The devil has armies of demons spread out over the whole earth. In certain areas, you will see wars, poverty, crimes, drugs, and prostitution—all kinds of spiritual wickedness. Understand that the devil is not like God. He is not omnipresent, so he uses demons and evil spirits to do his will.

> For we wrestle not against flesh and blood but against principalities against power against the rulers of the darkness of this world against spiritual wickedness in high places. (Ephesians 6:12)

As Christians, you must understand that the devil and his demons are real, and they are always ready to attack. So do not make it easy for them to trick you. When you open doors in your life through unforgiveness, disobedience, or any sinful behavior, you give the devil permission to attack you mentally, physically, and emotionally. Those are his tactics. The devil only has the power you give him; he will never be more powerful than God. When the enemy comes, let it not be because we gave him permission. Our mission is to resist the devil and shut down the works of the wicked one in our lives.

> Ye are of God, little children and have overcome them, because greater is he that is in you then he that is in the world. (1 John 4:4)

> For it is better, if it is the will of God, to suffer for doing good than for doing evil. (1 Peter 3:17)

Never be fooled by the devil's tricks. He is cunning and a deceiver. He will use people and temptations to cause havoc in the lives of the believers. He will use your weaknesses against you. So if you have any unresolved sins in your life, the devil will use it against you. For me, it was the lottery. Yes, I was a Christian buying lottery tickets every time I went to a store or gas station, and I had the nerve to pray over them and ask God to let me win. This went on for a while because I believed the lie of the enemy that told me that in order to be rich quick, I had to play to get the millions. The devil had me trying to use the scriptures for worldly gain. "But the wealth of the sinner is stored up for the righteous" (Proverbs 13:22). I had to repent for using God's word for worldly gain. I know that God will bless his children without using evil ways to get it.

> The blessings of the Lord makes one rich,
> And He adds no sorrow with it. (Proverbs 10:22)

> Wealth gained by dishonesty will be diminished, but he who gathers by labor will increase. (Proverbs 13:11)

God's blessings make one rich, not the lottery for believers of the Most High God. We are to put our trust in him; not gambling, casinos, lottery, or anything else that will take your focus off of God. We are not to love money so much that we are running after it, trying to get it at any cost.

> But my God shall supply all your needs according to his riches in Glory by Christ Jesus. (Philippians 4:19)

> For the LOVE of money is the root of all evil; which some coveted after, they have erred from the faith, and pierced themselves through with many sorrows. (Timothy 6:10)

These two scriptures opened my eyes because I was in love with and coveting after money. All I thought about was how to get money; I did not trust God. I was not relying on him to meet my needs as a single mother with two children. Once I realized that I must trust God for everything and not trust in the lottery, palm readers, horoscope, astrology, or anything that would take my focus off of the Lord. What the enemy wants to do is have you so detached and distracted that you miss God's blessings. The only way to defeat your enemy is by staying in and using the word of God. Jesus was tempted by the devil and he resisted him by using the word of God. If Jesus used the word, why do you think you can defeat the devil any other way?

Discussed your thoughts for the chapter and write your own prayer.

# Part 5

# The Steps

# Chapter 5

# Walking by Faith

What is *faith*? It is a blind knowing: I don't see it, but I know it is coming. As it says in Corinthians 5:7, "For we walk by faith, not by sight."

Walking by faith was very hard for me in the beginning. I had some faith as we all do—the kind of faith that if I sit in a chair, I won't fall on the floor. I was a born-again believer struggling with my faith, walking with God every single day. I was unable to trust his word for my life. I tried to believe in the Word, but I was full of doubt and unbelief and that hindered me from receiving from him.

> But let him ask in faith, with no doubting, for he who doubts is like a wave of the sea driven and tossed by the wind. For let not that man suppose that he will receive anything from the Lord; he is a double-minded man, unstable in all his ways. (James 1:6–8)

I learned that there is no other way to walk with God but by faith, and faith is the key that will unlock your happiness. God has given all of us a measure of faith that we must build upon every day. We cannot operate in fear, which is the opposite of faith that the devil puts on the children of God to keep them from moving forward in their walk. Fear will block your faith. The only fear a believer should have is the reverential fear of the Lord God Almighty. Walking in faith is a form of trusting in God for everything.

> Trust in the Lord with all thine heart, and lean not unto thy own understanding. In all thy ways acknowledge Him, and He shall direct thy paths. (Proverbs 3:5–6)

Don't walk in little faith. Continue to build on it every day and stay in the Word of God. That will increase your faith and watch all the miracles that go on around you. When your relationship with the Lord becomes closer and closer, your intimacy with the Father will increase, and you will begin to trust him and know that he will take care of you. With trust comes faith, a blind knowing: I don't see it, but I know God will bring it to pass.

## Power and Authority

> And Stephen, full of faith and power, did great wonders and miracles among the people. (Acts 6:8)

Just as Stephen had faith and power, we, as believers, have it too. But many Christians don't believe; they have it or know how to walk in their power and authority. We can speak things into existence, and we can decree and declare things to come to pass. When Jesus died on the cross for the sins of the world, he died for our sins, so we don't have to, and we are to do the same things that Jesus did when he walked upon the earth. He told you to go forth, preach, teach, and make disciples of men. When Jesus told the twelve disciples to go forth, he gave them power.

> And when He had called His twelve disciples to Him, He gave them power over unclean spirits, to cast them out, and to heal all kinds of sickness and all kinds of disease. (Matthew 10:1)

## IT'S THAT EASY

You are the disciples of Jesus Christ, and you too have power and authority to enforce spiritual laws that are in the Word of God. You are to speak the promises of God over every situation in your life and to expect results. You are the seed of Abraham. When God made Abraham a promise that will continue to his seeds down through each generation of believers, that means you can walk with confidence and boldness. You can speak God's word and watch it come to pass.

> For assuredly, I say to you, whoever says to this mountain, Be removed and be cast into the sea, and does not doubt in his heart, but believes that those things he says will be done, he will have whatever he says. (Mark 11:23)

I know there will still be some struggling Christians who are still living in doubt and unbelief that the Word does not apply to the Christians of today but was only for those back then. My question to you would be, "Why would Jesus have had to die on the cross for people who lived over two thousand years ago and not for us today?" We are their descendants, and when he died for their sins, ours were included. So that qualified you to walk in all the power and authority that was given to them.

> Believe Me that I am in the Father and the Father in Me, or else believe Me for the sake of the works themselves. Most assuredly, I say to you, he who believes in Me, the works that I do he will do also; and greater works than these he will do, because I go to My Father. (John 14:11–12)

The believers can do all that Jesus says. You can do by the power and authority that he has given to you by using his name. In order for you to enforce your power and authority, you must abide in Jesus; you can't do anything without him.

Learn what the laws of the kingdom of God are by reading the Bible; it will change your life as it changed mine. When I started speaking the Word over my situations, speaking his promises into my life and the lives of others, it was amazing to see how God moved. All I did was put him first in my life. Live out the process and let God handle everything and begin to transform your life.

> Abide in Me, and I in you, as the branch cannot bear fruit of itself, unless it abides in the vine, neither can you, unless you abide in Me. I am the vine, you are the branches. He who abides in Me, and I in him, bears much fruit; for without Me you can do nothing. (John 15:4–5)

## Victory

When you think of *victory* what comes to mind? Winning a race. Beating an opponent.

*Victory* is an act of defeating an enemy or opponent in a battle, game, or other competition.

In order to have victory in your Christian's walk, you must stay in the Word of God (Bible) because there is no other way to defeat the enemy (devil) but by using the Word, and if you don't read the Bible, how will you know what to say to your enemy? Just like the military has to prepare for battle, so do you.

> Wherefore take unto you the whole armor of God, that ye may be able to withstand in the evil day, and having done all to stand. (Ephesians 6:13)

For a Christian, what does the armor look like?

1. Loins girt about with *truth*
2. Breastplate of *righteousness*
3. Feet shod with the *gospel of peace*
4. Shield of *faith*
5. Helmet of *salvation*
6. Sword of the *spirit*

## IT'S THAT EASY

The armor we put on will always be found in the Word of God. When we do battle, the enemy (devil) can never defeat a child of God who comes to the fight fully prepared. Stay in the Word, meditate on it day and night, and hold on to your faith.

I was so happy to learn from my aunt how to read the Bible. She said, "Don't read it like a novel but go from book to book, chapter by chapter, and verse by verse, and discuss it with other believers to dig deep into it." And when I pray, I pray the Word over every situation, and when I praise and worship, I make sure I am sincere. When I repent for something I've done wrong, I am always prepared to change and turn away from it. Allow the Holy Spirit to direct your steps. He is there to lead and guide you.

Having the tools you need to walk in victory is the key to living a victorious life in Christ. Knowing who you are and belong to makes a difference in the life of the believer.

> You are of God, little children, and have overcome them, because He who is in you is greater than he who is in the world. (1 John 4:4)

> Finally, my brethren, be strong in the Lord and in the power of His might. (Ephesians 6:10)

Discussed your thoughts for the chapter and write your own prayer.

www.ingramcontent.com/pod-product-compliance
Lightning Source LLC
LaVergne TN
LVHW051123280125
802364LV00002B/310